Editor's Comment

Energy Infrastructures is the bedrock and key to ensuring global supply of oil and gas. This edition takes a look at the 13 largest pipeline operators in North America which delivers oil and gas to end users. In similar vein, the top five distribution hubs in North America that allow for quick and easy access to market is also featured.

The latest oil, gas and energy news around the globe is reported in this edition. Some energy saving tips on how to keep cool and save in this hot summer is discussed. Hence, this edition is a must read, our news content will convince you.

Our Event- The international pipeline, oil and gas safety conference March 14-16, 2017, POGS '17-Registration now Open and Call for Abstract still on going. Register Today @ http://oilandgassafetyconference.com

Recognition- Our Magazine is now one of the Best Sellers on Amazon in Petrochemical, Petroleum and Oil and Energy Categories.

- Gloria Towolawi

Contents

USA Oil and Gas Monitor
A RGT Media Communications Corp.

Editor-in-Chief
Gloria Towolawi

Europe Bureau
Esther Coker

Nigeria Bureau
David Arhavbarien

Contributing Editor
Gloria Instead

Reporter
Caleb Motinwo

Advert & Marketing
Jewel Spring
T: 832-486-0095
E: advertise@usaoilandgasmonitor.com

Distribution & sales
Richard Godfirst

Subscribers Service
E: subscribe@usaoilandgasmonitor.com

RGT Media Communications Corp.
Publishers of
USA Oil and Gas Monitor
Workplace Weekly News
GlobalPRPlus

USA Oil and Gas Monitor is published 12 times a year monthly by RGT Media Communications Corp. 10777 Westheimer #1100

Houston, Texas 77042
Subscription price is $144 per year.
Digital copy $9.99 per download.

August 2016 • Issue 8

U.S. Onshore Oil Companies Operating Cash Flow Improves

First-Quarter 2016 Financial Results

First-quarter 2016 financial results from U.S. onshore producers reveal an improving balance between capital expenditure and operating cash flow. Although operating cash flow was the lowest in any quarter in the past five years, larger reductions to capital expenditure brought these companies closest to self-finance when capital investment can be paid for entirely from operating cash flow. With crude oil prices such as the global benchmark Brent price averaging over $45 per barrel in the second quarter—a 34 per cent increase from first-quarter 2016—cash flow may improve and help offset declining revenue from lower production.

The difference between operating cash flow and capital expenditure—known as free cash flow or the financing gap—represents whether a company can pay for its investment through its after-tax profits. Over the past five years, companies substantially increased investment spending to raise production. In 2012 and early 2013, operating cash flow was about half of capital expenditure, making external finance necessary to pay for investment in production growth.

Although the crude oil price decline since 2014 has led to significant reductions in operating cash flow for U.S. oil companies, their immediate financial situations are improving. As oil companies' spending falls and crude oil prices increase, the need for oil companies to find external sources of funding may decline, which could reduce financial strain in the coming quarters.

Sources of cash that do not come from operating activities typically come from:
- Selling property, equipment, other business segments, or other assets
- Issuing shares of stock
- Taking on debt, such as through borrowing from a bank or selling a bond

Operating cash flow has declined over the past year, but it nonetheless has covered an increasing share of capital expenditure as companies are reducing their investment budgets more quickly. Smaller investment budgets are lowering the amount of cash U.S. onshore oil producers need to raise through outside sources.

Capital expenditure decreases, however, may lead to further declines in production for U.S. oil producers. First-quarter 2016 was the first year-over-year decline in crude oil and other liquids production for these companies in the past five years, driven by declines from existing fields and a lack of new well drilling. Falling production would likely reduce revenue and cash flow absent an increase in crude oil prices.

The companies included in this analysis according to EIA are: 39 public U.S. crude oil producers operating only onshore fields. Their collective production averaged 2.1 million barrels per day, or approximately 30 per cent of U.S. Lower 48 production in first-quarter 2016. These companies will release second-quarter 2016 results in mid-August.

India Poised to Grow Its Strategic Petroleum Reserve

India plans to bring online the country's first strategic petroleum reserve SPR, in response to India's increasing reliance on petroleum imports. The first phase of India's SPR includes three locations Visakhapatnam, Mangalore, and Padur, in southern India with a combined capacity of 39.1 million barrels of crude oil. The Visakhapatnam facility on the eastern coast began filling its underground caverns last summer.

Once filled, these three facilities would provide an estimated 13 days of net oil import coverage, based on 2015 consumption and production data.

India's ultimate goal is to have an SPR that provides 90 days of net import coverage. The Indian government unveiled plans to add another 91 million barrels of SPR capacity in a second phase by 2020, although these facilities are still in the planning phase. The Indian Strategic Petroleum Reserves Limited ISPRL, a special-purpose legal entity owned by the Oil Industry Development Board, would manage all of the SPR facilities.

The significant drop in international oil prices since mid-2014 provides India with an incentive to speed up construction and filling of its SPR. India is seeking to finance the second phase of its SPR partially through commercial agreements with foreign oil producers who can lease storage. India is currently negotiating with the United Arab Emirates' national oil company, ADNOC, to lease 5.5 million barrels of the Mangalore facility. Two-thirds of this volume would be available for India, and ADNOC could store the remaining volumes or sell the oil in the domestic market.

Other companies such as Kuwait Petroleum Corporation, Saudi Aramco, and Shell have also expressed interest in India's storage facilities. In February 2016, India proposed a federal income tax exemption for the sale of stored crude oil by foreign firms to the local market as an incentive for foreign oil companies to lease space, which in turn would help finance the SPR program. Relatively high current global oil inventories that have reduced available storage space could be another driver for crude oil producers to seek new storage capacity. Even though India has incentives for foreign investors to store crude oil in its SPR facilities, companies are waiting for regulatory issues to be settled, such as local taxes and India's ban on crude oil exports.

The gap between India's oil demand and supply is widening, with demand surging ahead. Based on EIA estimates, imports supplied 75 per cent of the country's total liquids demand, as India's total liquid fuels consumption in 2015 reached more than 4 million barrels per day b/d, compared with about 1 million b/d of total domestic liquids production.

Demand for crude oil and petroleum products in India is projected to continue climbing, further increasing the country's oil import dependence. In addition to India's rising consumption, filling the remainder of the country's first phase of its SPR will further increase demand. Although India has diversified its crude oil import slate in the past few years, adding imports from countries in Africa and Latin America, it still relies on Middle Eastern countries for most of these imports 58 per cent in 2015.

August 2016 • Issue 8

Natural Gas Flaring In North Dakota Has Declined Sharply Since 2014

Natural gas flaring in the United States is not confined to North Dakota, but since 2012, North Dakota has had the highest volumes of flared natural gas. By law, North Dakota prohibits natural gas venting. The volume of North Dakota's natural gas production that is flared has fallen sharply in both absolute and percentage terms since 2014. In March 2016, 10 per cent of North Dakota's total natural gas production was flared, less than one-third of the January 2014 flaring rate, which was at 36 per cent. Flaring rates and volumes have significantly decreased as North Dakota's total natural gas production has continued to grow, setting a monthly total natural gas production record of 1.71 billion cubic feet per day in March 2016. The North Dakota Industrial Commission established targets in September 2015 to reduce natural gas flaring.

Most North Dakota oil and natural gas production is in the Bakken formation, a relatively new production area that has lacked sufficient natural gas pipeline infrastructure. As new infrastructure has been built, more of the Bakken region's natural gas production has been brought to market, reducing the volume of flared natural gas despite much higher production.

New wells account for a large share of the volume of North Dakota's flared natural gas. North Dakota oil and gas regulations require that tax and royalties be paid for all natural gas flaring beyond a well's first year of production. The North Dakota Department of Mineral Resources can grant confidential reporting status to wells for the first six months of a well's production. These wells, which are also known as confidential wells, have nearly double the flaring rates of non-confidential wells.

Based on data for the 12 months from April 2015 through March 2016, 29 per cent of the natural gas produced by confidential wells in North Dakota was flared, while 15 per cent of the natural gas from non-confidential wells was flared. Once a well's first year of production ends, operators must cap the well, connect it to a natural gas gathering line, equip the well with an electrical generator that consumes at least 75 per cent of the natural gas from the well, or find another approved approach that reduces flaring.

The North Dakota Industrial Commission first established targets for the percentage of natural gas flared in April 2014 and subsequently revised these targets in September 2015. Currently, the targets allow a maximum of 23 per cent of production volumes to be flared through the first quarter of 2016, 20 per cent for April through October 2016, 15 per cent for November 2016 through October 2018, and 12 per cent for November 2018 through October 2020. Ultimately, the target falls to 9 per cent of production beginning November 1, 2020.

Natural gas is flared -burned rather than vented- released into the air- without combustion for both safety and environmental reasons. Vented, unprocessed natural gas contains hydrocarbons that are heavier than air, such as propane and butane, which can be hazardous if ignited. Methane, the primary component of natural gas, is also a potent greenhouse gas. Flaring natural gas produces carbon dioxide, which, while also a greenhouse gas, has a much lower global warming potential, a measure of how various gases can affect the atmosphere's radiative balance, than methane.

Golar and Schlumberger Form OneLNG Joint Venture

Golar LNG Limited "Golar" and Schlumberger today announced the creation of OneLNGSM, a joint venture to rapidly develop low cost gas reserves to LNG. The combination of Schlumberger reservoir knowledge, wellbore technologies and production management capabilities, with Golar's low cost FLNG Floating LNG solution, will offer gas resource owners a faster and lower cost development thereby increasing the net present value of the resources.

Golar and Schlumberger have 51/49 ownership of the joint venture. Golar and Schlumberger have agreed an initial investment commitment to cover the estimated equity needed to develop the first project. In addition, the parties will on a project-by-project basis discuss additional debt capital as required. This future financing will take into account Golar's FLNG intellectual property through an equitable contribution mechanism to be agreed between the parties.

Golar Vice Chairman, Tor Olav Troim said, "Our new venture with Schlumberger provides a powerful union of their oilfield services technology and production management business, and our low cost FLNG solution. It leverages Golar's LNG expertise, and builds upon our industry leading position as a midstream solutions provider."

Schlumberger, President Operations, Patrick Schorn commented, "This new joint venture is uniquely positioned to optimize the development of low cost gas reserves. The technology platform and production management capability that Schlumberger brings will enable a total system approach, leading to a simpler and fast-tracked FID process, and reliable operational execution for the benefit of the gas resource owners."

OneLNG will be the exclusive vehicle for all projects that involve the conversion of natural gas to LNG, which require both Schlumberger Production Management services and Golar's FLNG expertise. After reviewing the current market opportunities where 40 per cent of the world's gas reserves can be classified as stranded, both parties are excited at the future prospects of OneLNG and are confident that it would conclude 5 projects within the next 5 years. Golar LNG is one of the world's largest independent owners and operators of LNG carriers with over 30 years of experience. The company developed the world's first Floating Storage and Regasification Unit FSRU projects based on the conversion of existing LNG carriers. Our strategic objective is to become an integrated midstream player in the LNG industry.

Schlumberger is the world's leading provider of technology for reservoir characterization, drilling, production, and processing to the oil and gas industry. Working in more than 85 countries and employing approximately 100,000 people who represent over 140 nationalities, Schlumberger supplies the industry's most comprehensive range of products and services, from exploration through production, and integrated pore-to-pipeline solutions that optimize hydrocarbon recovery to deliver reservoir performance.

Schlumberger Limited has principal offices in Paris, Houston, London and The Hague, and reported revenues of $35.47 billion in 2015.

August 2016 • Issue 8

AEG Power Solutions to Supply Equipment Securing Power Supply in a Russian Gas Production Project in the Arctic

AEG Power Solutions, a global vendor of power supply systems and provider of industrial power supply and renewable energy solutions, today announced that it was awarded a contract to supply equipment that will be insuring uninterrupted power supply for the Yamal LNG Project Yamal-Nenets Autonomous Area, Russia. Protect 8 uninterrupted power supply systems by AEG PS meets all of the stringent technical requirements that Yamal LNG has set for the equipment to be operated in challenging climate conditions.

The Yamal LNG Plant will receive more than 50 Protect 8 three-phase UPS units 400 V AC in/384 V DC out. The Protect 8 UPS employs cutting-edge technology and is based on the double conversion topology. This technology is a robust and commercially beneficial solution to ensure safe operation of high-performance equipment in demanding climate conditions.

"We have a rich experience and the Protect 8 UPS system has a proven track record of operation in most challenging environments," said John Ferriman, Vice President for Global Industry Sales at AEG Power Solutions. "We are very glad to take part in such an ambitious project. The gas market is now gaining momentum and we are positioning ourselves to benefit from it," Mr. Ferriman added.

JSC Yamal LNG is implementing a project to build a natural gas liquefaction plant with a capacity of 16.5 MTPA based on the resources of the South-Tambeyskoye Field. The plant is to produce its first LNG in 2017. OAO NOVATEK with 50.1 per cent, Total 20 per cent, CNPC 20 per cent, and the Silk Road Fund 9.9 per cent are the shareholders of Yamal LNG.

US Congress Approves Use of Drones to Enhance Energy Infrastructure Safety

American Petroleum Institute Midstream Director Robin Rorick said making drone technology available to operators will help the industry achieve its goal of zero incidents. The Senate passed the Federal Aviation Administration Reauthorization with a provision that would allow unmanned aircraft system UAS utilization for oil and gas facilities, refineries, pipeline inspection, and response activities.

"Safety is our core value, and the best way to protect the public and the environment is to prevent incidents from ever happening," said Rorick. "Drone technology will complement the comprehensive safety practices that the industry has in place to ensure that all Americans continue to enjoy the affordable, reliable fuels they depend on.

"The ability to use drones will allow the industry to use the latest technologies to continue to effectively monitor infrastructure and facilities while minimizing the risk to personnel."

API thanked the Senate and the House for adopting this UAS provision and urged the president to quickly sign the legislation into law.

ExxonMobil to Acquire InterOil in Transaction worth More Than $2.5 Billion

ExxonMobil

- ExxonMobil to pay $45 per share plus additional cash payment based on Elk-Antelope resource size
- Boards of directors of both companies unanimously approve terms of agreement
- Acquisition adds to ExxonMobil resources in successful Papua New Guinea business
- Oil Search transaction terminated

Exxon Mobil Corporation NYSE: XOM and InterOil Corporation NYSE: IOC, POMSoX: IOC has announced an agreed transaction worth more than $2.5 billion, under which ExxonMobil will acquire all of the outstanding shares of InterOil, the ExxonMobil Transaction.

"This agreement will enable ExxonMobil to create value for the shareholders of both companies and the people of Papua New Guinea," said Rex W. Tillerson, chairman and chief executive officer of Exxon Mobil Corporation.

"InterOil's resources will enhance ExxonMobil's already successful business in Papua New Guinea and bolster the company's strong position in liquefied natural gas."

InterOil Chairman Chris Finlayson said, "Our board of directors thoroughly reviewed the ExxonMobil transaction and concluded that it delivers superior value to InterOil shareholders. They will also benefit from their interest in ExxonMobil's diverse asset base and dividend stream."

Under the terms of the agreement with ExxonMobil, InterOil shareholders will receive:

A payment of $45.00 per share of InterOil, paid in ExxonMobil shares, at closing. The number of ExxonMobil shares paid per share of InterOil will be calculated based on the volume weighted average price VWAP of ExxonMobil shares over a measuring period of 10 days ending shortly before the closing date Share Consideration.

A Contingent Resource Payment CRP, which will be an additional cash payment of $7.07 per share for each trillion cubic feet equivalent tcfe gross resource certification of the Elk-Antelope field above 6.2 tcfe, up to a maximum of 10 tcfe. The CRP will be paid on the completion of the interim certification process in accordance with the Share Purchase Agreement with Total SA, which will include the Antelope-7 appraisal well, scheduled to be drilled later in 2016. The CRP will not be transferrable and will not be listed on any exchange.

Together the Share Consideration and the CRP represent a material premium to the closing price of InterOil shares on May 19, 2016 -- the day prior to the announcement of the Oil Search transaction -- based on a range of Elk-Antelope resource estimates:

Tcfe	6.2	7.0	8.0	9.0	10.0
	(Base Volume)				(Cap)
Share Consideration Value	$ 45.00	$ 45.00	$ 45.00	$ 45.00	$ 45.00
CRP – Potential Value1	$ 0.00	$ 5.66	$ 12.73	$ 19.80	$ 26.87
Aggregate Consideration (US$/share)	$ 45.00	$ 50.66	$ 57.73	$ 64.80	$ 71.87
Premium to May 19 close 2	42.2 %	60.1 %	82.4 %	104.7 %	127.1 %
Premium to 1-month VWAP 3	41.2 %	58.9 %	81.1 %	103.2 %	125.4 %
Premium to 3-month VWAP 4	48.2 %	66.8 %	90.1 %	113.4 %	136.6

Compelling Benefits of the Transaction

When concluded, this transaction will give ExxonMobil access to InterOil's resource base, which includes interests in six licenses in Papua New Guinea covering about four million acres, including PRL 15. The Elk-Antelope field in PRL 15 is the anchor field for the proposed Papua LNG project.

ExxonMobil's more than 40 years of experience in the global LNG business enables it to efficiently link complex elements such as resource development, pipelines, liquefaction plants, shipping and regasification terminals, which it has demonstrated through the PNG LNG project, working closely with co-ventures', national, provincial and local governments, and local communities. ExxonMobil will bring to bear its industry-leading performance and strong commitment to excellence as it grows its business in Papua New Guinea.

August 2016 • Issue 8

The PNG LNG project, the first of its kind in the country, was developed by ExxonMobil in challenging conditions on budget and ahead of schedule and is now exceeding production design capacity, demonstrating the company's leadership in project management and operations.

ExxonMobil will work with co-ventures' and the government to evaluate processing of gas from the Elk-Antelope field by expanding the PNG LNG project. This would take advantage of synergies offered by expansion of an existing project to realize time and cost reductions that would benefit the PNG Treasury, the government's holding in Oil Search, other shareholders and landowners.

Path to Completion

The ExxonMobil Transaction has been unanimously approved by the boards of both companies. The InterOil board unanimously recommends that InterOil shareholders approve the ExxonMobil Transaction.

The ExxonMobil Transaction will be implemented by way of a court-approved plan of arrangement under the Business Corporations Act Yukon and will require the approval of at least 66 2/3 percent of the votes cast by InterOil shareholders at a special meeting expected to take place in September, 2016.

In addition to InterOil shareholder and court approvals, the ExxonMobil Transaction is also subject to other customary conditions. Subject to obtaining the aforementioned approvals and satisfaction of closing conditions, the ExxonMobil Transaction is expected to close in September, 2016.

Oil Search Transaction

The InterOil board of directors, in consultation with its independent legal and financial advisors, determined that the ExxonMobil Transaction is superior to the previously announced transaction with Oil Search Limited ASX:OSH, POMSoX: OSH and so advised Oil Search on July 18, 2016. Immediately prior to entering into the arrangement agreement with ExxonMobil, InterOil terminated its previously announced arrangement agreement with Oil Search, and ExxonMobil is paying Oil Search the termination fee in accordance with the requirements of the Oil Search arrangement agreement on behalf of InterOil. The previously scheduled Special Meeting of Shareholders to vote for the approval of the Oil Search transaction has been cancelled.

SABIC and ExxonMobil Evaluating Petrochemical Joint Venture on U.S. Gulf Coast

- Potential new complex would be located in Texas or Louisiana near natural gas feedstock
- Project would include a steam cracker and derivative units
- Plans in early stages, final investment decision to follow study completion

SABIC and an affiliate of Exxon Mobil Corporation ExxonMobil NYSE:XOM are considering the potential development of a jointly owned petrochemical complex on the U.S. Gulf Coast.

If developed, the project would be located in Texas or Louisiana near natural gas feedstock and include a world-scale steam cracker and derivative units.

Before making final investment decisions, the companies will conduct necessary studies and work with state and local officials to help identify a potential site with adequate infrastructure access.

"We are focused on geographic diversification to supply new markets," said Yousef Abdullah Al-Benyan, SABIC vice chairman and chief executive officer. "The proposed venture would capture competitive feedstock and reinforce SABIC's strong position in the value chain."

Neil Chapman, president of ExxonMobil Chemical Company, said: "We have the capability to design a project with a unique set of attributes that would make it competitive globally. That is vitally important as most of the chemical demand growth in the next several decades is anticipated to come from developing economies."

ExxonMobil and SABIC have worked together for 35 years in major chemical joint ventures in Saudi Arabia.

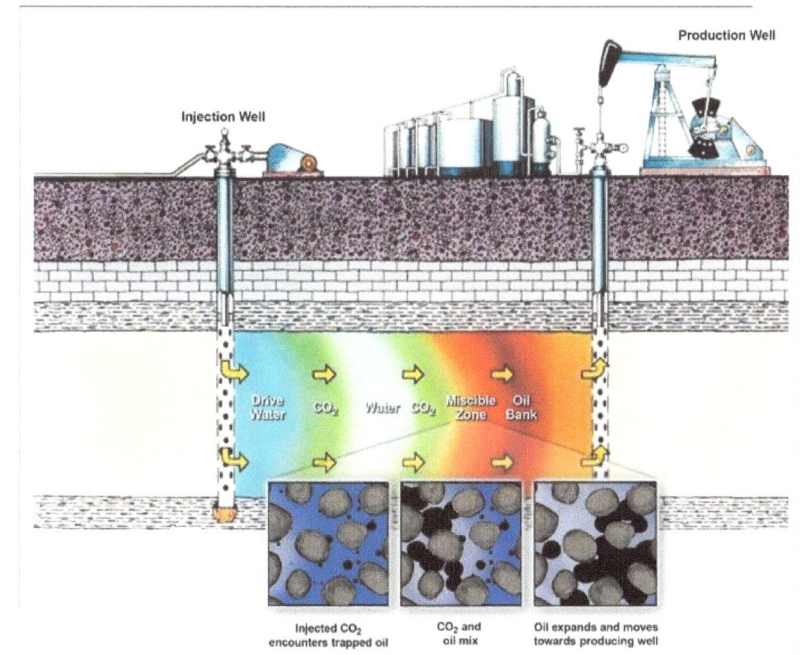

Air Products Successfully Captured 3 Millionth Metric Ton of CO2 for EOR

Allentown, PA-based Air Products successfully captured and transported, via pipeline, its 3 millionth metric ton of carbon dioxide CO2 to be used for enhanced oil recovery. This achievement highlights the ongoing success of a carbon capture and storage CCS project sponsored by the U.S. Department of Energy DOE and managed by the National Energy Technology Laboratory NETL.

The project demonstrates how a gas separation technology called vacuum swing adsorption can be implemented into an operating facility. The technology is being used at a hydrogen production facility in Port Arthur, Texas, to capture more than 90 percent of the CO2 from the product streams of two commercial-scale steam methane reformers, preventing its release into the atmosphere.

In addition to demonstrating the integration of Air Products' vacuum swing adsorption technology, the project is also helping to verify that CO2-enhanced oil recovery CO2-EOR is an effective method for permanently storing CO2. CO2-EOR allows CO2 to be stored safely and permanently in geologic formations, while increasing oil production from fields once thought to be exhausted.

The CO2 captured from the Port Arthur facility is being used for EOR at the West Hastings Unit oilfield in southeast Texas. Injected CO2 is able to dissolve and displace oil residue that is trapped in rock pores. It is estimated that the West Hastings Unit could produce between 60 and 90 million additional barrels of oil using CO2 injection.

In total, projects sponsored by the U.S. Department of Energy have captured and securely stored more than 12 million metric tons of CO2, equivalent to taking more than 2 million cars off the road for a year. Investing in projects and technologies, such as Air Products', are critical to paving the way for more widespread use of CCS technologies.

The Air Products project is supported through DOE's Industrial Carbon Capture and Storage ICCS program, which is advancing the deployment of CCS technologies for industrial sources at commercial and utility-scale. CCS innovation is important to not only reduce future greenhouse gas emissions from power plants, but it also helps to ensure that U.S. industries are powered in the most efficient, sustainable, and clean way possible, while continuing to use America's long-standing and abundant energy resources.

August 2016 • Issue 8

Middle East and Recovering Flows in Nigeria Consolidate OPEC Market Share

OPEC crude output rose by 400 kb/d in June to an eight-year high of 33.21 mb/d, including newly re-joined Gabon. Saudi Arabia ramped up to a near-record rate of 10.45 mb/d and Nigerian flows partially recovered. Middle East producers sustained record pumping rates, consolidating market share and pushing OPEC's total output 510 kb/d above one year ago.

Global oil supplies rose by 0.6 mb/d in June, to 96 mb/d, after outages curbed OPEC and non-OPEC supplies in May, while production was 750 kb/d below as higher OPEC output only partially offset non-OPEC declines, the newly released IEA Oil Market Report OMR for July informs subscribers. Non-OPEC supplies are set to decline by 0.9 mb/d in 2016, to 56.5 mb/d, before rising 0.2 mb/d in 2017.

Robust European demand supported second quarter

2016 global demand growth at around 1.4 mb/d year-on-year, momentum that will be roughly matched through the year as a whole. A modest deceleration is foreseen in 2017, as growth eases to 1.3 mb/d taking average deliveries up to 97.4 mb/d.

Crude oil prices eased from an early June peak above $52/bbl, but traded within a $45-$50/bbl range. Growing uncertainty over the global economy and the related dollar strength weighed, but the downside was limited by further declines in US production and inventories.

OECD commercial inventories built by 13.5 mb in May to end the month at a record 3 074 mb. Preliminary information for June suggest that OECD stocks added a further 0.9 mb while floating storage has continued to build, reaching its highest level since 2009.

May global refinery throughput plunged by almost 1 mb/d from April, to 1.5 mb/d year-on-year, as heavy outages took their toll in many regions. This lowered the second quarter estimate for global refinery intake to 78.54 mb/d – the first year-on-year drop in three years. The forecast for third quarter throughput is more steady at 80.95 mb/d.

U.S.-China EcoPartnership to Make Coal Power Plants Cleaner

The U.S. and China has announced six new EcoPartnerships during the recent U.S.-China Strategic and Economic Dialogue in Beijing, China. Among the new partnerships is a collaboration between Alabama-based Chemical and Metal Technologies CMT and China's CPI Yuanda Environmental Protection Engineering Company. CPI Yuanda is a subsidiary of State Power Investment Corporation SPIC, one of China's largest generating power companies.

The CMT-CPI Yuanda partnership will evaluate CMT's new cleanup technology for removing heavy metals from industrial wastewater produced during capture of sulfur dioxide in a post-combustion flue gas desulphurization FGD unit. The technology will be tested at SPIC's Hechuan Flue Gas Comprehensive Experimental Base's 2 x 300 MW coal-fired power plant in Chongqing, China. A successful demonstration of CMT's technology for wastewater cleanup would be followed by a demonstration of the technology for flue gas treatment.

CMT has developed a sorbent to treat flue gas and wastewater from coal-burning power plants to remove mercury, heavy metals, selenium, and nitrates/nitrites. The technology is expected to meet, or exceed, the U.S. Environmental Protection Agency's regulations for wastewater. The technology has received third-party validation at lab scale in the U.S. The goal of the Yuanda demonstration is to clean the FGD wastewater to meet drinking water standards, which exceeds China's current requirements.

The partnership between CMT and CPI Yuanda is a direct result of the companies' participation in the recent Mercury and Fine Particulate Emission Control Workshop held under the joint Annex I: Power Generation and Annex IV: Energy & Environmental Technologies of the U.S.-China Fossil Energy Protocol FEP.

The FEP is part of a broader, ongoing effort between the U.S. Department of Energy and China's Ministry of Science and Technology to promote clean energy research and development on fossil energy technologies. This partnership includes the U.S.-China Clean Energy Research Center, which facilitates U.S.-China collaboration on clean energy technology R&D, including carbon capture, utilization and storage CCUS technologies.

August 2016 • Issue 8

ExxonMobil to Expand Ultra-Low Sulfur Fuels Production at Beaumont Refinery

ExxonMobil

- Production of ultra-low sulfur diesel and gasoline to expand by more than 40,000 barrels per day
- Proprietary technology removes sulfur and yields product with minimal octane loss
- Investment will ensure gasoline meets latest environmental standards

ExxonMobil has announced plans to increase production of ultra-low sulfur fuels at its Beaumont refinery by approximately 40,000 barrels per day, further strengthening its integrated downstream portfolio while meeting environmental standards.

Construction is scheduled during the second half of 2016 to install a selective cat naphtha hydrofining unit, which uses a proprietary catalyst system to remove sulfur while minimizing octane loss. Startup of the flexible technology, known as SCANfining, is expected in 2018. Gasoline produced using this technology will meet the U.S. Environmental Protection Agency's Tier 3 gasoline sulfur specifications.

"ExxonMobil continues to strengthen its portfolio of world-class refining assets," said Steve Cope, director of North America refining, for ExxonMobil. "This investment further enhances the competitiveness of our U.S. Gulf Coast refineries."

Installation of the selective cat naphtha hydrofining unit is the facility's second expansion project in a year, following the announcement of the Beaumont refinery's capacity expansion in 2015, and demonstrates ExxonMobil's long-term view and disciplined approach toward advantaged business investments. Beaumont is well positioned to competitively supply high-demand growth markets around the U.S. in the face of a challenging industry environment.

"This specialized unit will improve our product yield, and demonstrates our technology advantage and focus on increasing energy efficiency," said Fernando Salazar, manager of the Beaumont refinery. "This project represents the largest capital investment in our Beaumont refinery operations in more than a decade, and will benefit the local economy with both temporary and full-time jobs."

ExxonMobil Refining and Supply and its stewarded affiliates operate a global network of reliable and efficient manufacturing plants, transportation systems, and distribution centers that provide a range of fuels, lubricants, and other high-value products and feedstocks to our customers around the world.

ExxonMobil's Beaumont refinery is part of the company's integrated operations in Beaumont, Texas, which includes a 345,000 barrel-per-day capacity refinery, as well as chemical, lubricants and polyethylene plants. ExxonMobil has approximately 2,100 area employees, and its operations account for approximately 1 in every 7 jobs in the region. A 20,000 barrel-per-day expansion of the refinery's crude processing ability, announced in 2015, is currently under way.

July 2016 • Issue 7

LNG Canada's Joint Venture Participants Delay Timing of Final Investment Decision

LNG Canada announces that its joint venture participants – Shell, PetroChina, Mitsubishi Corporation and Kogas – have decided to delay a final investment decision on LNG Canada that was planned for end 2016.

LNG Canada remains a promising opportunity – it has strong stakeholder and First Nations' support, has achieved critical regulatory approvals, has important commercial and engineering contracts in place to design and build the project, and through its pipeline partner Coastal Gas Link, has received necessary environmental approvals and First Nations support along the pipeline right-of-way.

"Our project has benefitted from the overwhelming support of the BC Government, First Nations – in particular the Haisla, and the Kitimat community. We could not have advanced the project thus far without it. I can't say enough about how valuable this support has been and how important it will be as we look at a range of options to move the project forward towards a positive FID by the Joint Venture participants," said Andy Calitz, CEO LNG Canada.

Through their efforts to build a strong LNG sector for Canada, and a critical, cleaner energy alternative for the world, the governments of British Columbia and Canada have developed sound fiscal and regulatory frameworks for success.

However, in the context of global industry challenges, including capital constraints, the LNG Canada Joint Venture participants have determined they need more time prior to taking a final investment decision. At this time, we cannot confirm when this decision will be made.

LNG Canada will continue key site preparation activities and work with its joint venture participants, partners, stakeholders and First Nations to define a revised path forward to FID.

LNG Canada Joint Venture Participants are Shell 50 per cent, PetroChina 20 per cent, Mitsubishi Corporation 15 per cent and Kogas 15 per cent.

August 2016 • Issue 8

Top Five North America's Distribution Hubs

Southern California

The southern California hub is the top gateway for trade between the United States and Asia. It supports over a million jobs nationally and generates billions of dollars in economic activity each year.

Port of Los Angeles and Long Beach Port puts Southern California as the number one container port and leader in container volume and cargo value in North America and world's ninth-busiest port complex by container volume, after Shanghai, Singapore, Shenzhen China, Hong Kong, Busan S. Korea, Ningbo China, Qingdao China and Guangzhou China.

Lehigh Valley

Lehigh Valley is a two-county region in eastern Pennsylvania. Located one hour north of Philadelphia and west of New York City. Port Newark/Elizabeth Marine Terminal NJ/NY
Port of Philadelphia. Lehigh Valley International Airport, Newark Liberty International Airport, and Philadelphia International Airport. The region enjoys quick access to three major interstates – I-78 East/West, I-80 East/West and the Pennsylvania Turnpike's Northeast Extension North/South – as well as easy access to the ports of Philadelphia, New Jersey, and New York, and light commuter traffic to our downtowns and industrial parks. Located within one day's drive of one-third of all U.S. consumers, and half of all Canadian consumers.

Texas

DALLAS-FORT WORTH, HOUSTON INTERCONTINENTAL, PORT OF HOUSTON, TEXAS CITY, CORPUS CHRISTI, BROWNSVILLE, HIDALGO-MCALLEN, LAREDO, EAGLE PASS and EL PASO. These ports aid quick logistics and distribution decision- making Texas the third largest distribution hub in North America.

In 2011, Texas ranked as the top state for exports for the tenth consecutive year, with a total of $251 billion worth of goods shipped internationally. The state's top export commodities in 2011 were

petroleum and coal products, chemicals, computer and electronic products, machinery, and transportation equipment. Mexico was Texas' top export destination in 2011, followed by Canada, main-land China, Brazil, and the Netherlands.

Toronto

Toronto benefits from Canada's strong trade relationships, including the historic North American Free Trade Agreement NAFTA, which created the largest free trade zone in the world, and shares proximity and time zone with the world's largest concentration of economic activity - the northeastern United States. European and Asian markets also offer tremendous trade opportunities.

The city lies within a 90-minute flight of New York, Chicago, Boston, Philadelphia, Pittsburgh and Washington. Accordingly, Toronto benefits from an impressive network of road, rail, sea, and air links that help move the province's exports, half of which are generated in the city. Modern network of highways and transcontinental railway lines that traverse the city, local businesses are also well served by two airports, including Pearson International Airport, the largest in Canada. In addition to moving cargo, Pearson International Airport offers non-stop and same-plane service on scheduled and chartered flights to over 180 destinations around the globe.

Chicago

Intermodal yard is the main reason Chicago remains one of the key transportation hubs in North America. They are critical in efficiently connecting manufacturers and farmers across the Midwest to domestic and foreign markets. Simone Weil, senior policy analyst at the Chicago Metropolitan Agency for Planning said, "We have over $3 trillion moving through the region each year. That's trillion with a T, not billion. The intermodal yards play an important role in that". Chicago is just the one place where all the railroads meet, and it's a big end market.

The Chicago area is also home to O'Hare Airport which supports major air freight operations. The area also has two other major airports; Chicago Midway International Airport and Gary Airport. Inbound and outbound freight volumes by air are projected to increase at a faster rate than truck and rail well into 2040.

August 2016 • Issue 8

Thirteen Largest U.S. Interstate Natural Gas Pipeline Operators Ranked by System Capacity

Operators	System Capacity- MMcf/d
Kinder Morgan	28,518
TransCanada	27,085
Williams	13,416
Spectra Energy Group	10,679
Energy Transfer Partners, L.P	10,521
Boardwalk Pipeline Partners, LP	10,325
Berkshire Hathaway Energy	9,275
Dominion Transmission Co.	6,655
Center Point Energy	5,385
Questar Pipeline Co.	3,192
Southern Star Central Pipeline Co.	2,801
National Fuel Gas Supply Co.	2,312
Enbridge, US	2,053

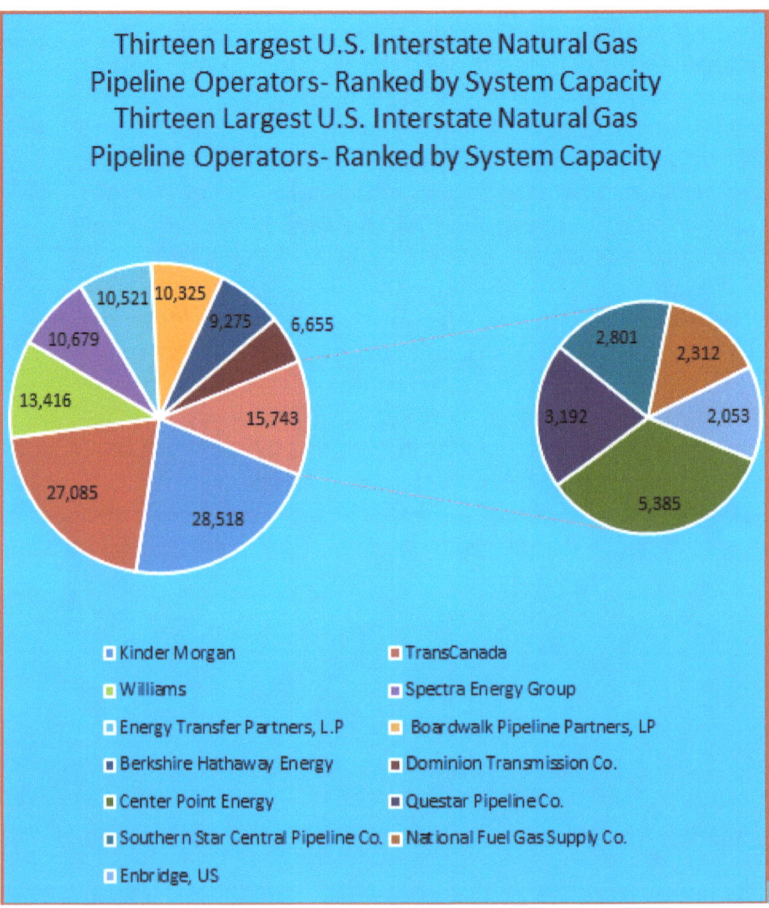

Regulatory Impact on Fuel Consumption and Greenhouse Gas Emissions Phase 2 Standards for Medium- and Heavy-Duty Vehicles- shows reduction in Diesel consumption

The transportation sector is the second-largest consumer of energy in the United States, accounting for more than 70 per cent of U.S. petroleum consumption and thus playing a significant role in projections of energy demand. The Annual Energy Outlook 2016 AEO2016 Reference case reflects the effects of existing laws and regulations on the fuel consumption and greenhouse gas GHG emissions of medium- and heavy-duty vehicles, which in 2015 accounted for 20 per cent of total energy consumption in the transportation sector and 60 per cent of total delivered distillate fuel consumption.

EIA has produced a separate case—the Phase 2 Standards case—to analyze the impacts of a proposed rulemaking jointly issued by the U.S. Environmental Protection Agency EPA and the National Highway Traffic Safety Administration NHTSA in July 2015 [1] The proposed standards build on the Phase 1 GHG emissions standards for medium-duty vehicles MDVs and heavy-duty vehicles HDVs that were implemented starting in model year MY 2014. The proposed Phase 2 rulemaking establishes a second round of standards for GHG emissions and fuel con-sumption by medium- and heavy-duty trucks. The Phase 1 standards extend through MY 2018. The proposed Phase 2 standards take effect in MY 2021 or MY 2018 for trailers and increase in stringency through MY 2027.

In the AEO2016 Phase 2 Standards case, average fuel economy increases for all new vehicles covered by the standards. In 2040, total MDV and HDV energy consumption, which is 3.4 million barrels per day oil equivalent in the AEO2016 Reference case, is 2.6 million barrels per day oil equivalent in the Phase 2 Standards case, or 22 per cent lower. Total MDV and HDV diesel fuel use in 2040 is 18% lower than in the Reference case. With higher on-road fuel economy of the truck stock in the Phase 2 Standards case, total delivered energy consumption in the transporta-tion sector is 6% lower in 2040 than in the Reference case. As the average fuel economy of conventional vehicles increases in the Phase 2 Standards case, there is also less incentive to pay high capital costs for natural gas and propane vehicles despite their lower fuel costs, and there is a shift away from natural gas and propane toward conventional diesel and gasoline fuels.

The proposed Phase 2 standards address specific vehicle categories, including combination tractors, trailers, heavy-duty HD pickup trucks and vans, and vocational vehicles Table IF2-1. For combination

August 2016 • Issue 8

tractors, standards are proposed by cab, roof, and fuel type. In addition, for the first time, standards are proposed for heavy-haul tractors and for trailers pulled by Class 7 and Class 8 tractors. The proposed standards for trailers vary in stringency, depending on the type of trailer. For HD pickups and vans, the proposed standards are categorized by diesel or gasoline engine and are set as total gallons consumed per 100 miles or as grams per mile. For heavy-duty pickups and vans, the proposed standards consider a vehicle's work factor—the weighted aver-age of payload and towing capacity. For vocational vehicles, the proposed standards are based on chassis type, gross vehicle weight rating GVWR, engine type, and drive cycle.

The AEO2016 Phase 2 Standards case analyzes the estimated effects of the proposed regula-tions on fuel consumption and GHG emissions. The requirements for each of the vehicle categories are derived from U.S. Energy Information Administration projected sales, distributed into the size classes according to data from Polk Automotive and the U.S. Census Bureau's Vehicle Inventory and Use Survey VIUS.

Vehicle Category	Description	Truck classes covered
Combination tractors	Semi-trucks that typically pull trailers	Class 7 and Class 8 GVWR 26,001 pounds and above
Heavy-duty pickups and vans	Pickup trucks and vans, such as 3/4-ton or 1-ton pickups for exam-ple used on construction sites or 12- to 15-person passenger vans	Class 2b and Class 3 GVWR 8,501 to 14,000 pounds
Vocational vehicles	Wide range of truck configura-tions, such as delivery, refuse, utility, dump, cement, school bus, ambulance, and tow trucks. For purposes of the rulemaking, vocational vehicles are defined as all heavy-duty trucks that are not combination tractors or heavy-du-ty pickups or vans	Class 2b through Class 8 GVWR 8,501 pounds and above

Table IF2-1. Types of vehicles regulated by the proposed Phase 2 standards

Heavy-duty pickups and vans
The proposed standards for heavy-duty pickups and vans in Class 2b GVWR between 8,501 and 10,000 pounds and Class 3 GVWR between 10,001 and 14,000 pounds are phased in from MY 2021 to MY 2027. Although heavy-duty pickups and vans often use efficiency improvements similar to those for light-duty pickup trucks and vans, the standards are based on a work-based metric rather than on the footprint metric used for light-duty vehicles. The work factor incorporates towing and payload capacity as well as four-wheel drive capability in determining

minimum fuel efficiency requirements.

The proposed standards include an annual 2.5 per cent per year reduction in allowable emissions from MY 2021 to MY 2027, an approximate 16 per cent increase from the standards set by Phase 1 for MY 2018. Standards are set individually for vehicles with spark ignition engines and vehicles with compression ignition engines, but the standards are expected to improve at the same rate. Compliance test procedures for heavy-duty pickups and vans employ the same EPA drive cycles used to determine light-duty vehicle compliance, and manufacturer compliance retains the same Phase 1 production-weighted fleet average to determine compliance.

Combination tractor cabs
The proposed Phase 2 standards continue the attribute-based classification of combination trac-tor cabs from Phase 1—by Classes 7 and 8, day and sleeper cabs, and roof height low, mid, high. In addition, a specific set of vocational tractors, heavy-haul tractors, are subject to a specific standard to reflect their unique powertrains. The proposed standards would require reduc-tions in carbon dioxide CO_2 emissions and fuel consumption of up to 24 per cent com-pared to the MY 2017 baseline. They are based on expected technology improvements for engines, transmissions, drivelines, aerodynamics, tires, accessories, and extended idle reduction technologies. Tractors are certified with the Greenhouse Gas Emissions Model GEM.

Trailers
The contributions of trailers to fuel efficiency improvement are not regulated in Phase 1. The proposed Phase 2 standards apply to trailers pulled by Classes 7 and 8 tractors coupled to the fifth wheel. The most comprehensive requirements are applicable to traditional long-box trailers, both refrigerated and dry, which typically are pulled by high-roof cab tractors. **The proposed changes center on improving aerodynamics and reducing rolling resistance. Compliance is determined with a version of GEM.** The standards are less stringent for trailer categories with shorter boxes or trailers with aerodynamic limitations. Non-box trailers and non-aerodynamic box vans are required to adopt

specific tire technologies to comply. In total, there are 10 separate categories:

- Long-box dry vans longer than 50 feet
- Long-box refrigerated vans longer than 50 feet
- Short-box dry vans 50 feet and shorter
- Short-box refrigerated vans 50 feet and shorter
- Partial-aero long-box dry vans
- Partial-aero long-box refrigerated vans
- Partial-aero short-box dry vans
- Partial-aero short-box refrigerated vans
- Non-aero box vans all lengths of dry and refrigerated vans
- Non-box trailers tanker, platform, container chassis, and all other types of highway trailers that are not box trailers.

With the exception of refrigerated units, trailers typically do not directly emit GHGs. However, the proposed standards assign required levels of emissions and fuel consumption as if the trailers were pulled by a standard reference tractor. The standards require reductions of 3 per cent to 8 per cent from MY 2021 to MY 2027 in fuel consumption and CO_2 emissions, depending on the trailer type. Certain trailers are exempt, including those that operate only at low speed and those that are used for logging and mining. Trailers are also certified with GEM.

Vocational vehicles

Vocational vehicles are separated into three class groups: light heavy-duty Classes 2b–5, medi-um heavy-duty Classes 6–7, and heavy heavy-duty Class 8. Each class group is separated by engine type compression or spark ignition and a duty cycle that captures expected vehicle usage and energy consumption. The three available duty cycles are urban, multi-purpose, and regional. Because power requirements for vocational vehicles vary widely, multiple baseline drivelines are available in the Phase 2 standards for calculating fuel efficiency and GHG emission improvements. Standards are set at increments starting in MY 2021, with updates in MY 2024 and MY 2027.

In comparison with MY 2017 baseline vehicles, the proposed standards require a 16 per cent reduction in CO_2 emissions and fuel consumption for all vehicles across all weight classes powered by compression ignition primarily diesel engines. Vocational vehicles powered by spark ignition engines are subject to emission and fuel-use reductions by MY 2027 of 12

per cent for light heavy-duty, 13 per cent for medium heavy-duty, and 12 per cent for heavy heavy-duty. Like combination tractors and trailers, vocational vehicles are certified with GEM.

Certification for combination tractors, trailers, and vocational vehicles

As in Phase 1, compliance for tractors and vocational vehicles is certified in Phase 2 using an updated version of GEM that incorporates some fixed input values, such as payload and trailer weights, to determine fuel efficiency performance by drive cycle. Compliance can be achieved through adoption of various technology combinations. Improving on Phase 1, the Phase 2 GEM incorporates several changes to more accurately reflect the effects of technology adoption on fuel efficiency performance. These changes include road grade, an additional averaged aerodynamic drag coefficient, and improved simulation of engines and transmissions. Ultimately, the changes mean that a vehicle evaluated with the Phase 2 GEM would have higher CO_2 emissions and fuel consumption than if evaluated with the Phase 1 GEM. Consequently, results from the two standards are not directly comparable. Trailers are modeled in GEM with attribute inputs for aerodynamics, tires, weight characteristics, and performance.

Results

The Phase 2 Standards case estimates fuel efficiency improvement and fuel consumption based on the proposed requirements for combination tractors, HD pickups and vans, and vocational vehicles. Trailer stocks are not explicitly modeled, because there are limited data on trailer inven-tories and usage; however, efficiency improvements as a result of the adoption of limited trailer improvements are included in the model. Between MY 2017 and MY 2027, the Phase 2 Stand-ards case indicates that the proposed standards lead to the

August 2016 • Issue 8

adoption of technologies to improve fuel economy that otherwise would not have been purchased. Although the standards do not start until MY 2021, manufacturers are expected to begin adoption beforehand to ensure initial compliance by MY 2021. Fuel economy and energy usage reports combine vocational and non-vocational vehicles for Classes 3, 4–6, and 7–8.

New vehicle average fuel economy increases for all size classes in the Phase 2 Standards case. From 2017 to 2027, new vehicle average fuel economy combined Classes 3–8 rises by 28 per cent in the Phase 2 Standards case compared to the Reference case. After 2027 the standards are held constant, but technology adoption continues as new technologies become available. In 2040, new vehicle fuel efficiency averages 10.6 miles per gallon gasoline equivalent in the Phase 2 Standards case, representing a 33 per cent improvement compared to the Reference case. The improvements represent over compliance as the model continues to adopt cost-effective technologies beyond 2027.

The increase in fuel economy of the entire vehicle stock is lagged, reflecting slow turnover in the stock of Classes 2b–8 trucks, which have a median lifetime of 12 years. As new medium- and heavy-duty trucks are added to the total stock, and older trucks with lower fuel economy are removed from service, the average on-road fuel economy for the total stock of heavy-duty trucks increases in the Phase 2 Standards case Figure IF2-1.

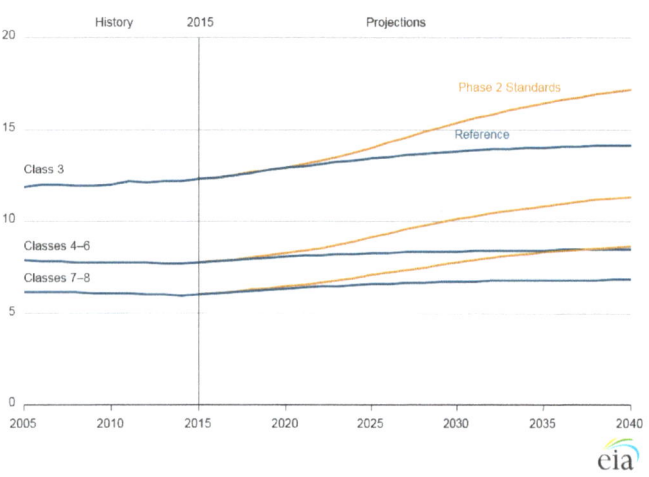

Figure IF2-1. Average on-road fuel economy of vehicles by weight class, 2005–40

miles per gallon gasoline equivalent

In comparison with the AEO2016 Reference case, differences in total vehicle sales and stocks are negligible in the Phase 2 Standards case. Between 2017 and 2040, new MDV and HDV sales per year are equal to about 5% of the total truck stock, ranging from about 660,000 to 790,000 new MDV and HDV sales per year out of a total stock that grows from 11.7 million in 2017 to 17.2 million in 2040. However, there is a shift away from

natural gas and propane toward conventional diesel and gasoline in the Phase 2 Standards case. As the average fuel economy of conventional vehicles increases, there is less incentive to pay high capital costs for natural gas and propane vehicles, despite their lower fuel costs.

The most significant effect of Phase 2 is a reduction of diesel consumption—the most commonly used fuel—in medium- and heavy-duty vehicles. In the Reference case, MDV and HDV diesel consumption increases steadily through 2040, as industrial output grows Figure IF2-2. In the Phase 2 Standards case, diesel consumption decreases from 2015 to 2033 as gains in fuel economy more than offset growth in transport requirements. After 2033, diesel consumption increases slowly without continued enhancement of the standard, but in 2040 it still is 18 per cent lower in the Phase 2 Standards case than in the Reference case. Cumulative MDV and HDV consumption of diesel fuel from 2021 to 2040 in the Phase 2 Standards case is 2.5 billion barrels lower than in the Reference case.

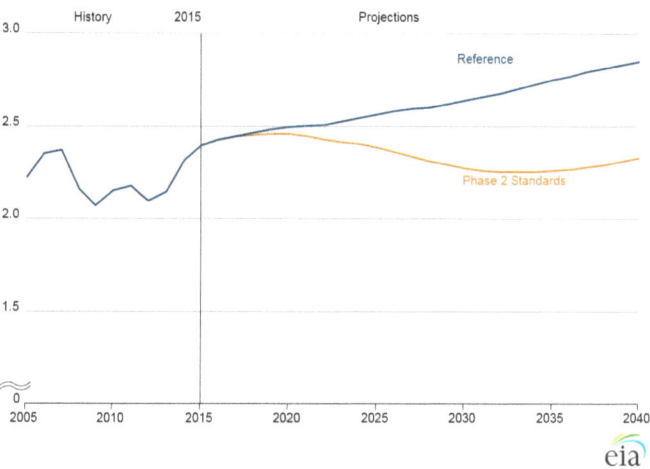

Figure IF2-2. Diesel fuel consumption by large trucks, Classes 3-8, in two cases, 2005-40

million barrels per day

The reduction in diesel consumption in the Phase 2 Standards case has significant implications for the mix, as well as the amount, of petroleum products consumed in the United States. Implications for refiners would depend on the extent to which similar standards were adopted in other countries with significant trucking activity, because diesel and other petroleum products are widely traded in global markets.

Consumption of other fuels by MDVs and HDVs—including gasoline, propane, liquefied natural gas LNG, and compressed natural gas CNG—is lower in the Phase 2 Standards case than in the Reference case Figure IF2-3. In the Phase 2 Standards case, diesel fuel consumption accounts for 90 per cent of all fuel consumption by MDVs and HDVs in 2040, with the remainder consisting primarily of gasoline and a small amount of natural gas. The higher diesel share in the Phase 2 Standards case reflects a shift away from alternative fuels as improved fuel economy reduces the incentive to pay high capital costs for natural gas and propane vehicles despite their lower fuel costs.

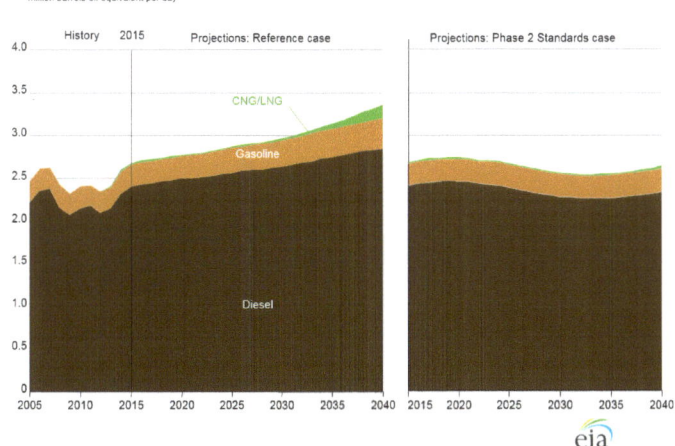

Figure IF2-3. Fuel consumption by large trucks, Classes 3–8, in two cases, 2005–40

million barrels oil equivalent per day

In the Phase 2 Standards case, higher on-road fuel economy of the truck stock reduces total delivered energy consumption in the transportation sector. From 2021 to 2040, cumulative delivered energy consumption in the transportation sector is 3 per cent lower in the Phase 2 Standards case than in the Reference case, and total transportation sector energy consumption in 2040 is about 750,000 barrels per day oil equivalent 22 per cent lower than in the Reference case Figure IF2-4. Cumulative CO_2 emissions from 2021 to 2040 in the transportation sector are 1,200 million metric tons 3 per cent lower in the Phase 2 Standards case than in the AEO2016 Reference case. In 2040, total transportation sector CO_2 emissions are 6 per cent lower in the Phase 2 Standards case than in the AEO2016 Reference case Figure IF2-5.

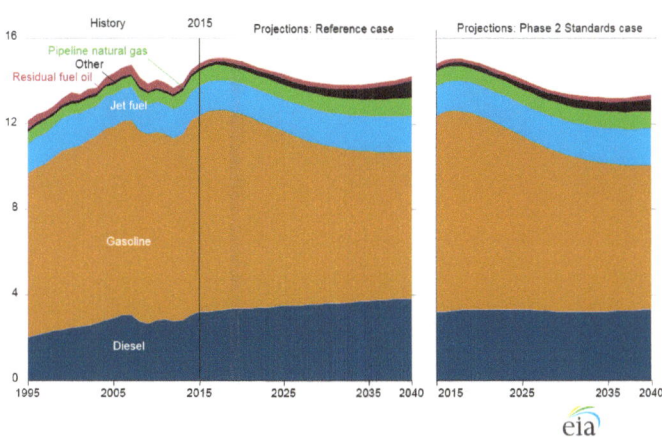

Figure IF2-4. Transportation sector energy consumption by fuel in two cases, 1995–2040

million barrels per day oil equivalent

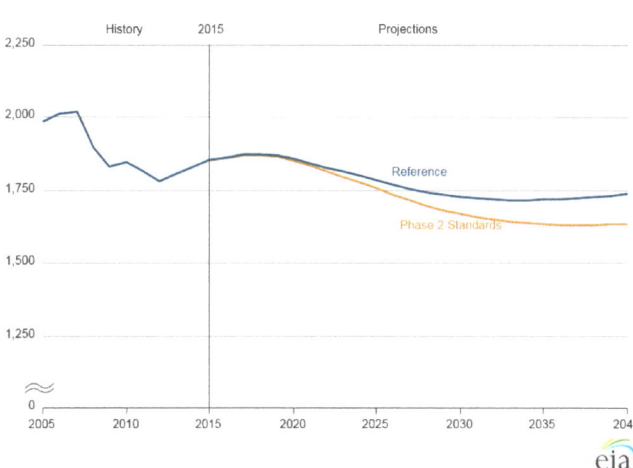

Figure IF2-5. Transportation sector carbon dioxide emissions in two cases, 2005–40

million metric tons

Regulatory and data limitations

- Although Class 2b pickup trucks and vans are included in the Phase 2 Standards case, their fuel economy and consumption are not reported individually. However, the effects of Class 2b are included in total transportation fuel consumption and emissions data.

- The Phase 2 Standards case approximates the proposed rulemaking by disaggregating Class 7 and Class 8 tractor vehicle body types based on data from the VIUS survey, which has not been updated since 2002. As a result, there may be significant differences between the tractor market today and more than a decade ago. Further, there are data uncertainties associated with vehicle usage reported in the VIUS survey. Nevertheless, the data were used because VIUS is the only source of information on tractor type.

- Trailers were not explicitly modeled in this study, because there are limited data on trailer inventories and usage. There are more registered trailers than tractors, and an understanding of usage logistics is critical to evaluating the adoption and overall results of improving trailer technology.

- Despite improvements since the start of Phase 1, there are still limits on data about the technologies used to meet the Phase 1 compliance standards. Consequently, it is difficult to esti-mate the energy outcomes that could be expected as medium- and heavy-duty trucks begin to comply with the new Phase 2 standards. Without better data, it is difficult to analyze the com-position of the truck market at the level of diversity included in the proposed standards, or the efficiency and fuel economy metrics associated with each classification in the standards.

- A critical issue is the limited availability of information that would provide a baseline from which to measure improvement. The lack of

August 2016 • Issue 8

baseline data is a result of the previously discussed data limitations, as well as operational changes in Phase 2 compared with Phase 1. Although many improvements have been made in GEM, the changes evaluation methods for the different technology categories make it difficult to map Phase 1 compliance to Phase 2. The baseline for Phase 2 MY 2017 assumes compliance with Phase 1 at that time, and it is evaluated differently. As a result, it is not known whether Phase 1 compliant vehicles in MY 2017 accurately represent the proposed Phase 2 baseline.

- Continuing issues from Phase 1 include how compliance will be measured and how well compliance testing procedures will replicate the average real-world performance of combination tractors, heavy-duty pickups and vans, vocational vehicles, and trailers. Phase 2 has three vo-cational drive cycles that can be used for compliance

urban, multi-purpose, and regional. Only the multi-purpose cycle is used in the AEO2016 Phase 2 Standards case. GEM has many new categories and improvements compared with Phase 1, but many of the categories are simplified to Yes or No responses, rather than to custom inputs. Some inputs, including payload and trailer weights, are fixed.

- Compliance for heavy-duty pickups and vans will be determined by a vehicle test procedure similar to that used in the national program for light-duty vehicles, including the highway fuel economy test and the federal test procedure for city driving, weighted 45 per cent and 55 per cent, respectively. Heavy-duty pickups and vans are assumed to be loaded to one-half of their payload capacity.

EN 14236
Evaluation
Certification
OIML R 137

Upgrading of the evaluation certification of Sensirion`s gas meter modules to natural gas type L

Earlier this year, the gas meter modules SGM70xx from the leading Swiss sensor manufacturer Sensirion have achieved an evaluation certification in accordance with the harmonized standards EN 14236 and OIML R 137 for natural gas type H. This evaluation certification was now upgraded to natural gas type L. The evaluation certificate makes it easier and faster for gas meter manufactur-ers to obtain MID approval for gas meters using the SGM70xx sensor module as core metrological unit.

Sensirion as the leading manufacturer of microthermal gas meter modules has recently launched the standard product SGM70xx, which is highly suitable for use in smart gas meters. So far, over 500'000 residential and industrial gas meters have been installed in the field in Italy and Germany using Sensirion microthermal gas flow technology. At the beginning of this year, the gas meter modules SGM70xx achieved an evaluation certification in accordance with the harmonized standards EN 14236 and OIML R 137 for natural gas type H. This evaluation certification by NMi was now upgraded to the natural gas type L. NMi is one of the leading notified bodies in Europe for type approval examination and certification of measuring instruments with an independent ISO 17025 accreditation. The evaluation certificate makes it easier and faster for gas meter manufacturers to obtain MID approval for gas meters using the SGM70xx sensor module as core metrological unit.

Sensirion's certified SGM70xx standard products are available for class 1.5 type G1.6, G2.5, G4 and G6 gas meters, and feature high reliability, long-term stability, and resistance to contamination. The compact design, the low power consumption and the digital I2C interface allow easy integration and handling into gas meters. Sensirion gas meter modules are temperature-compensated and pressure independent, and are fully calibrated for air and natural gas.

About Sensirion AG

Sensirion AG, headquartered in Staefa, Switzerland, is the world's leading manufacturer of digital microsensors and systems. The product range includes humidity and temperature sensors, mass flow controllers, gas and liquid flow sensors, and differential pressure sensors. An international network with sales offices in the USA, Germany, China, Taiwan, Japan and Korea supplies international OEM customers with tailor-made sensor system solutions for a vast range of applications. Among other things, these include analytical instruments, consumer goods and automobiles, as well as the medical and HVAC industries. One of the hallmark features of Sensirion products is the use of patented CMOSens® Technology. CMOS-based sensor elements and systems permit intelligent system integration, including calibration and a digital interface. Sensirion's credentials as a reliable OEM supplier are underscored by its ISO/TS 16949 certification.

August 2016 • Issue 8

Curry Supply Expands Parts Distribution

Curry Supply Company, a worldwide manufacturer and distributor of commercial service vehicles, is significantly expanding their parts and components distribution network.

Construction is nearly complete on their main parts distribution facility in East Freedom, Pennsylvania to add an additional 32,000 sq. ft. of available warehouse and office space capacity. This expansion will allow for a much larger in-stock parts inventory. A multi-million dollar OEM replacement parts inventory is maintained for all makes and models of on- and off-road water trucks, mechanics trucks fuel/lube trucks, lube trucks, rail gear trucks, vacuum trucks, winch trucks, dump trucks, crash attenuator trucks, lube trailers, and lube skids.

The expanded two-story facility will also provide more customer and employee parking and allow easier access for walk-in customers. The expansion of this facility is expected to be completed late-summer 2016.

To service customers in the west and southwest, the company has begun stocking a comprehensive inventory of on- and off-road water truck parts at their new facility in the Houston, Texas area. Parts are available for most makes and models of water trucks.

Walk-in customers are welcome, or can be ordered by calling the 24-hour Houston Parts Hotline: 832-821-7222. The Curry Supply facility outside Houston is located at 1113 Howard Ave., Deer Park, TX.

The company continues to stock and sell their products and parts at Coleman's Equipment, their authorized dealer in Australia.

"We have experienced exceptional growth over the past few years," said Jason Ritchey, President. "With that type of growth, it is imperative that we provide an industry-leading level of post-sale support to our customers. Hence the need to expand our facilities to house an even greater volume of replacement parts."

Curry Supply Company is a family-owned business that was established in 1932. Over the past 84 years, Curry Supply has grown into one of America's largest manufacturers and dealers of commer-cial service vehicles including on- and off road water trucks, mechanics trucks, on- and off-road fuel/lube trucks, vacuum trucks, winch trucks, dump trucks, crash attenuator trucks, and lube skids. Curry Supply delivers internationally, with sales, parts, and service provided throughout the United States and Australia.

Chevron and JOVO Sign LNG Agreement

Chevron Corporation NYSE:CVX has announced that its wholly-owned subsidiary, Chevron U.S.A. Inc., has signed a Key Terms Agreement with Singapore Carbon Hydrogen Energy Pte. Ltd., a subsidiary of JOVO, for the delivery of liquefied natural gas LNG from Chevron's global supply portfolio. When the LNG Sale and Purchase Agreement is finalized, JOVO is expected to receive up to 0.5 million metric tons per annum of LNG over five years, with the first delivery expected to arrive in 2018.

"This agreement is another important step in the commercialization of Chevron's natural gas hold-ings," said Mike Wirth, executive vice president, Chevron Midstream and Development. "We are positioned to become one of the top 10 LNG suppliers in the world."

JOVO is a privately-owned Chinese energy company. Its LNG business portfolio includes a LNG receiving terminal, tank truck operations, urban pipelines for natural gas, automobile gas refilling stations, direct industrial clients, power plant customers and exclusive management of an industrial park in South China.

Savannah Sees First Vessel through Expanded Panama Canal

The MOL Benefactor is the first vessel to call on Savannah through the new locks of the expanded Panama Canal. At a capacity of 10,100 twenty-foot equivalent container units, the Benefactor is also the largest ship ever to call the Port of Savannah.

The massive container ship, scheduled to move over 3,000 containers at GPA's Garden City terminal, is also the first Savannah call of the G6 Alliance's new NYX service. The East Coast rotation of the new service includes the ports of New York/New Jersey, Virginia and Savannah, exclusively deploying vessels in the 10,000-TEU range.

"The arrival of the MOL Benefactor today ushers in a new era of larger vessels and services that will increase capacity, volumes and economic opportunities for Georgia and this region," said Griff Lynch, GPA's Executive Director. "GPA is well-positioned to handle the larger vessels and greater volumes due to the scale and scope of our operations."

With eight new neo-panamax cranes on order, GPA will have a total of 30 ship-to-shore cranes by 2018. GPA has also added 30 rubber-tired gantry cranes – used to handle containers on terminal – for a current fleet of 146 machines – the most of any single container terminal in the U.S. "Over the next six months to a year, we expect a higher ratio of 8,000- to 10,000-TEU container ships among our vessels calls. Within two years, we expect market shifts to send 12,000-TEU vessels to the U.S. East Coast," Lynch added.

To better accommodate the larger vessels via water, the Savannah Harbor Expansion Project (SHEP) will deepen the inner harbor to 47 feet and the outer harbor to 49 feet at mean low water. The outer portion of the harbor is now 15 percent complete with work progressing daily.

The Benefactor's next stop is Manzanillo International Terminal in Panama.

Georgia's deep-water ports and inland barge terminals support more than 369,000 jobs throughout the state annually and contribute $20.4 billion in income, $84.1 billion in revenue and $2.3 billion in state and local taxes to Georgia's economy. The Port of Savannah handled 8.2 percent of the U.S. containerized cargo volume and 10.3 percent of all U.S. containerized exports in CY2015.

August 2016 • Issue 8

Natural Gas Will Play a Growing Role in a Gradually Decarbonizing Energy System- CEDIGAZ

CEDIGAZ, the International Association for Natural Gas Information, has just released its Medium and Long Term Natural Gas Outlook 2016. This scenario, which incorporates key objectives of current and also planned national energy policies, highlights the growing role of natural gas as a bridge fuel towards a long-term increasingly renewable-based, efficient and sustainable energy system. Given the vast low-cost coal resources, the future expansion of natural gas in the global energy mix will be driven by the implementation of energy and environmental policies aiming to shift away from coal and oil to cleaner fuels within the context of a gradually decarbonizing electricity system. In this scenario, the future global natural gas expansion is supported by strong supply growth, particularly of unconventional gas and LNG, in a context of rising prices as energy markets re-balance. **CEDIGAZ Scenario's trajectory is on a 3°C path, with energy-related CO2 emissions increasing by 0.3 per cent /year on average, reaching almost 35 Gt over the 2030-2035 period.**

Natural gas demand is projected to grow by 1.6 per cent /year over 2014-2035, driven by emerging markets, where natural gas is making substantial inroads in power generation and industry.

Looking forward to 2035, the total primary energy consumption is forecast to grow at a moderate rate of 1 per cent /year in a context of increased energy efficiency. Global energy intensity is forecast to decline by 2.5 per cent / year - 4.5 per cent /year in China.

In this context, gas stands as the fastest-growing fossil fuel over 2014-2035 + 1.6 per cent /year. In contrast, the growth of oil and coal is expected to slow sharply, with respective annual rates of 0.2 per cent and 0.1 per cent. We see major Improvement in the sustainability of supply as wind and solar are the fastest growing fuel sources through 2035 + 8 per cent /year. China alone explains a quarter of their expansion, followed by the US and Europe.

Natural gas will increase its relative share in the global primary energy supply from 21.4 per cent in 2013 to 23.9 per cent in 2035. The trend decline in oil share continues, as oil is backed out from power generation and the manufactured industry. After expanding since 2000, coal share reverses down and gradually declines to reach parity with gas by the end of the projection period. The share of renewables rises substantially but is capped by their intermittency.

The pace of gas demand growth has been revised downwards compared with Outlook 2015. INDCs ahead of COP21 have been taken into account, meaning greater efforts to meet environmental goals via the deployment of renewables and increasingly efficient technologies. In Europe in particular, the 2030 Climate and Energy Package leaves little room for gas demand growth in volume terms. However, the share of gas in the power generation mix progresses at the expense of coal against the background of the rise of renewables.

Virtually all of the additional energy is consumed in emerging economies and 85 per cent of gas growth come from emerging economies. The US is the only industrialized market to record a significant growth in gas consumption in volume terms, thanks to the competitiveness of shale gas and the adoption of the Clean Power Plan.

China and the Middle East lead the way in gas demand growth, accounting for respectively 27 per cent and 25 per cent of the incremental volume over the projection period.

The power sector remains the main powerhouse behind gas expansion. Natural gas makes substantial inroads into the power generation mix in China, the US, Russia, the Middle East and Africa in particular.

Substantial growth in gas use in the manufactured Industry is also expected in the Middle East, China, India, Latin America, Southeast Asia, and also the US. Natural gas supply is driven by the US shale gas, Asia-Oceania unconventional gas and the Middle East

Natural gas production is expected to grow everywhere, with the exception of Europe - 2 per cent /year.

The main centers of gas production growth are the Middle East Iran, Asia China, Australia and the US shale gas.

On the national scale, the US, China, Iran, Australia and Russia are expected to show the largest production gains.

On emerging markets, implementing regulatory and price reforms is critical to boost investments in E&P including unconventional gas.

Unconventional gas will provide more than two-thirds of global additional supply and will account for 34 per cent of global gas output in 2035, up from 20 per cent in 2014.

Outside North America, unconventional gas growth will be concentrated in China, Australia and, to a lesser extent, Argentina. Unconventional development elsewhere will be small and slow due to public opposition Europe, and economic and environmental challenges. Interregional trade will account for an increasing share of global supply

Net interregional long distance trade is forecast to grow by 2.7 per cent /year from 398 bcm in 2014 to 690 bcm in 2035, due to Asia's post-2020 and Europe's growing import dependence.

Interregional pipeline flows grow by 2 per cent /year, boosted by Central Asia and Russia's exports to Asia, mainly China. With 30 per cent of its total gas import being Russian, Europe will remain strongly dependent on Russian gas, which will maintain its competitiveness.

LNG increases more rapidly than pipeline gas after 2020. International LNG trade is set to increase by 3.4 per cent /year to 2035. The share of LNG in interregional flows will progress from 47 per cent in 2014 to 53 per cent in 2035. In Europe, LNG will play a fast-growing role to ensure a flexible, secure, diversified and optimized supply portfolio.

North America emerges as a large-scale exporter, covering 18 per cent of total net interregional exports by 2035, at the expense of the Middle East and the CIS.

LNG will lead to a growing internationalization of gas markets with flexible LNG and hub pricing expanding in Europe and Asia, supported by US LNG.

In CEDIGAZ Scenario, the availability of low-cost US shale gas resources will be gradually restricted in the long term, leaving space for some other international LNG projects Canada, East Africa underpinned by fully or partially oil-indexed long term contracts.

Five Quick Ways to Save Energy on Home Cooling

It's hot out there! With temperatures reaching nearly triple digits in many parts of the country, air conditioning systems are working extra hard to keep you cool. While air conditioners provide comfort, they also use a lot of power. The Energy Information Administration estimates cooling accounts for about 6 percent of the total energy used in average American households -- costing consumers about $11 billion a year!

Here are some simple steps you can take to stay cool and save energy on hot summer days:

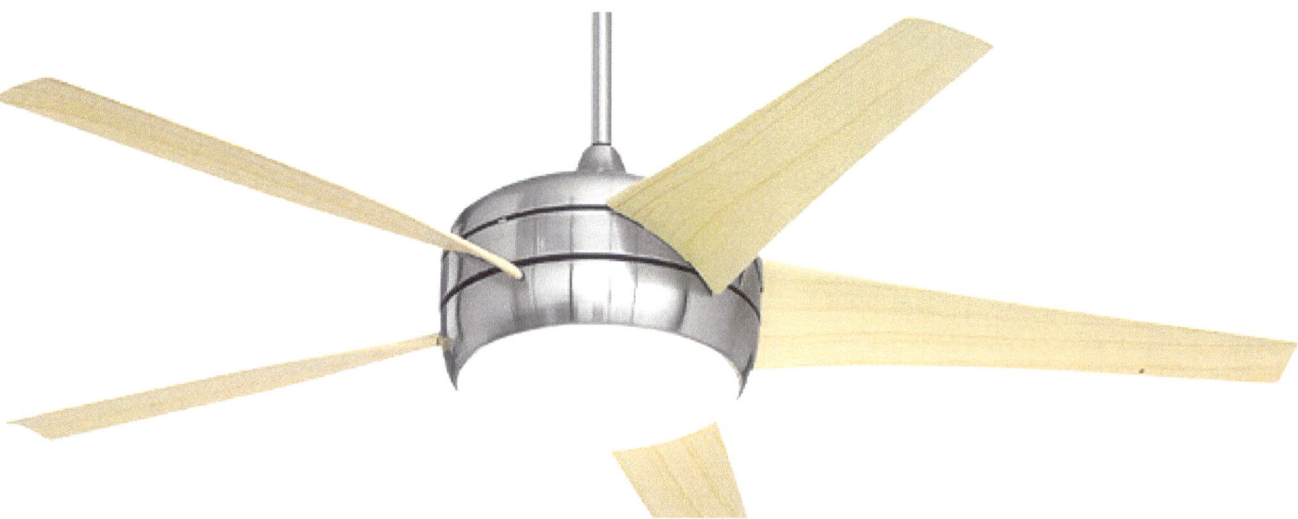

1. BECOME A FAN OF FANS.

For central air conditioning systems, a ceiling fan will allow you to raise the thermostat setting about 4 degrees Fahrenheit without sacrificing comfort. If you have a window air conditioner unit, try using a fan nearby to spread cooler air to other parts of the room and house.

2. MAINTAIN YOUR EQUIPMENT.

When was the last time you swapped out your air conditioner filter? Routinely replacing the filter could lower your air conditioner's energy consumption 5 to 15 percent. Even with filters, your system's evaporator coils can sometimes collect dirt. Check and clean these to help improve airflow.

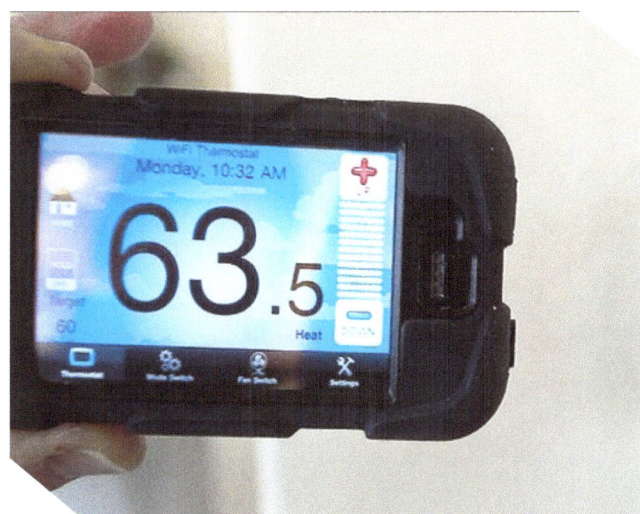

3. SET THAT THERMOSTAT.

When it comes to home cooling, every degree matters. You could save 10 percent a year on cooling costs by turning your thermostat up 7 to 10 degrees from its normal cooling setting for just eight hours a day. The smaller the difference between the indoor and outdoor temperatures, the lower your overall cooling bill will be.

4. SEAL THOSE CRACKS.

Keeping warm air out is crucial to staying cool on summer days. Check for any cracks around the edges of windows and doors and apply caulk or weatherstripping to seal them up.

5. BLOCK OUT THE SUN.

When you're outside, shade is a welcome respite from the glaring hot summer sun. The same can be said for the inside of your home. Energy efficient window treatments like blinds can block sunlight and keep the heat out. Highly reflective blinds can slash heat gain about 45 percent when totally closed and lowered.

www.ingramcontent.com/pod-product-compliance
Lightning Source LLC
Chambersburg PA
CBHW050423180526
45159CB00005B/2381